LIAR, LIAR, PANTS ON FIRE

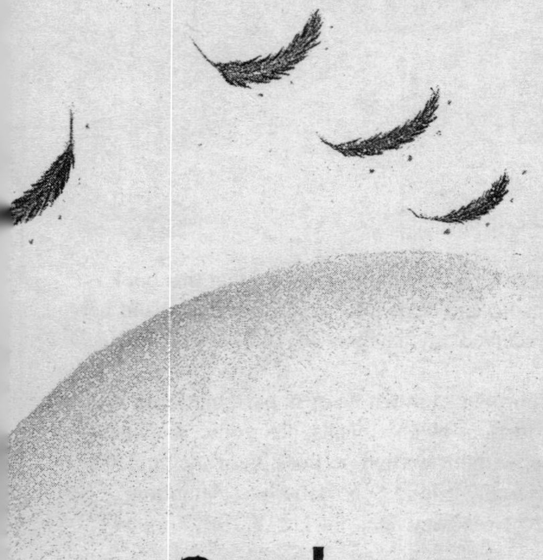

LIAR, LIAR, PANTS ON FIRE

Gordon Korman

illustrated by JoAnn Adinolfi

A
LITTLE APPLE
PAPERBACK

SCHOLASTIC INC.
New York Toronto London Auckland Sydney
Mexico City New Delhi Hong Kong

ISBN 0-590-27141-5

12 11 10 9 8 7 6 5 4 3 2 1 9/9 0 1 2 3 4/0

Printed in the U.S.A. 40

First Scholastic trade paperback printing, January 1999

The display type was set in Farmhause.
The text type was set in 16 point Bembo.
Book design by Marijka Kostiw

For Mrs. Korman's
third-grade class

Table of Contents

chapter one
The Nuclear Toilet

Check it out.

The school bell rang.

This wasn't a bad thing. It rang every day. But today it rang from half a block away. I was late.

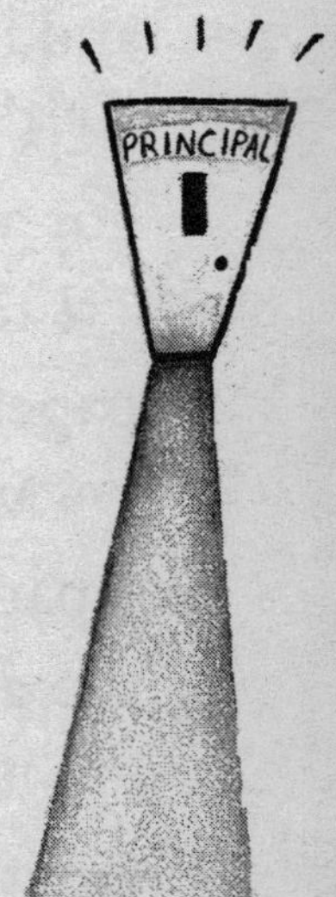

By the time I got to school, everyone else was pledging allegiance. I pledged along with them while I ran down the hall. It sounded more like huffing and puffing and gasping and wheezing. But it was really pledging.

I caught up to Jerry Paradise just outside our third-grade classroom.

He sneered at me. "Boy, Zoe. Are you ever in trouble!"

"Me?" I said. "You're as late as I am!"

When Jerry has something on you, he goes ballistic. He bounces up and down, and his voice gets high-pitched, like a bird's.

"I've got an excuse!" chirped Jerry. "I've got a note! Mrs. Moore! Mrs. Moore!"

I followed him into class. He pushed the paper right up to Mrs. Moore's face.

"My dad just left on a business trip to Japan," he announced. "So I got to go to the airport to say good-bye."

Our teacher read the note. "What an exciting trip," she told Jerry.

Then she turned to me. "And how about you, Zoe? Why weren't you in class when the bell rang?"

I frowned. It's pretty easy to tell the truth

when your dad takes airplane trips to amazing faraway places.

"Check it out," I began. "I was on the bus —"

"You walk to school!" squawked Jerry.

"I was *walking* to school," I re-started, "and I met this really famous movie star."

"Oh, wow!" cried Brittany Sanders. "Which one?"

Oops. Brittany knew about all the actors, and their clothes designers, and what kind of cars they drove. Her mom used to be a fashion model. I had to be careful.

"He made me promise not to say," I replied in a low voice. "If too many people find out there's a movie star in our town, he'll get mobbed."

"Liar, liar, pants on fire!" cried Jerry.

What a baby. Jerry talked like a two-year-old sometimes.

"Anyway," I went on, "I was getting his

autograph, but his pen was out of ink. And neither of us had enough money to buy a new one."

"If he's so famous, how come he isn't rich, too?" piped up Kevin Richards.

"Oh, he *is,*" I explained. "But he was wearing a giant banana suit for his new movie, and it didn't have any pockets. So I had to be an actor in the movie."

Jerry stared at me. "What for?"

"For the *money,*" I told him. "So I could buy the pen, and get his autograph."

"Let's see it," put in Brittany.

"That's the craziest part," I said quickly. "Just when I gave him the pen, he got this rare hand disease. Now he can't write anymore."

Mrs. Moore touched my arm and looked at me with concern. "Your sweater is soaking wet. What happened?"

PE

"Oh," I said, "I got my sleeve caught in the nuclear toilet."

The whole class gasped.

Mrs. Moore's eyes shot sparks. "Zoe Bent, how many times have we spoken about you making up wild stories?"

"But it's *true!*" I protested. "Our house has a nuclear toilet."

"That's enough, young lady!" she barked at me. "You've wasted too much of this class's time already. You're going to take a little walk. . . . You know where!"

Okay, so maybe I made up all that stuff about the movie star in the banana suit. But we did — we really *did* have a nuclear toilet.

There were two bathrooms in our house. The upstairs one was totally normal. But the downstairs one had a flusher like an atomic bomb.

First, you'd hear a rumbling sound like

distant thunder. Then fifty zillion gallons of water would flush through the bowl like Niagara Falls.

My grandpa was the first one who decided it was nuclear. He had just flushed his false teeth down by accident. The plumbing company said the teeth were nowhere in the neighborhood. Maybe not in the entire city.

I was *lucky* that all I got was a wet sleeve. The nuclear toilet could have sucked down my whole sweater. And me with it!

So now, whenever Grandpa came to visit, it was always the same. He would throw up his arms like a circus ringmaster and cry, "Let's have a look at the world's one and only nuclear toilet!"

Then he would take my little brother, Joey, into the living room and ask him a bunch of really hard questions. And Joey would get almost all of them right.

Joey was kind of a mini-genius. He got nothing but straight A's in school. He was only a first grader, but he could already do sixth-grade math.

"You'll be the next Albert Einstein," Grandpa promised Joey over and over.

Albert Einstein was this super-smart guy. I'd never heard of him, but Joey sure had.

One time I told Grandpa, "I happen to be the greatest third-grade geography expert in the universe. Did you know that East Dakota is the capital of Oshkosh, and Virginia is named after the first woman to climb up the North Pole?"

Grandpa looked at me and sighed. "The North Pole isn't like a telephone pole. You can't climb it. Maybe you should get your facts straight, sweetie. Take Joey, here. When's the last time you heard a lie from him?"

Well, it's easy to tell the truth when

you're a six-year-old genius. I mean, the only special thing about me was that I lived in a house with a nuclear toilet.

And I couldn't even talk about *that* without ending up exactly where I didn't want to be — walking down that long hall with no windows.

The scariest hall in the school.

I gulped. The door was humongous! Just looking at the top of it made my neck hurt. The pain got worse when I saw the gold lettering: PRINCIPAL.

I took a deep breath and knocked as softly as I could.

"Come in."

I pushed open the heavy oak door and stepped inside.

chapter two

Caramel Popcorn

I expected Dr. Bradley to be even madder than Mrs. Moore. But he didn't yell, or even look mean. Instead, he gave me a handful of brand-new pencils.

"It would be a big help, Zoe," he said, "if you could sharpen these."

I went to work at the sharpener, but I was totally confused. Didn't he know I was supposed to be in trouble? And how could a guy get to be the boss of an entire school if he didn't even know how to sharpen his own pencils?

Finally, I couldn't stand it anymore. "I can't get a detention," I blurted out. "I'm a volunteer firefighter. What if somebody's house bursts into flames right at three-thirty?"

Dr. Bradley got up from his desk and handed me an envelope. "Zoe, this is a note I'd like you to take home with you today."

Oh, no. "I'm in big trouble, aren't I?"

The principal looked serious. "Not if you remember to give it *only* to your father."

I frowned. "Why can't I show Mom?" Not that I wanted to show it to anybody. Principal's letters were automatic bad news. It was a law.

Dr. Bradley smiled. "When I was a fourth-grade teacher, I had a student with

THE LETTER HOME

the most fantastic imagination. His name was David Bent."

I goggled. "Dad?"

Wow. I knew Dr. Bradley was old — but not *that* old!

The principal nodded. "Oh, the tall tales that came from that boy — he was born on a cruise ship; his mother was a parachute jumper; his father was ambassador to India —"

I was amazed. "Grandma used to jump out of airplanes?"

Dr. Bradley shook his head. "It was all made up. Every last word."

I nodded. "Mom says Dad is a natural storyteller."

The principal took the sharpened pencils from me and put them on his desk. Then he asked, "Can you think of another natural storyteller we both know?"

Some grown-ups must think that kids

are total idiots. I knew Dr. Bradley wanted me to say, "Oh, yes. It's me, and I've learned my lesson. I'll never lie again."

He just didn't understand. I didn't stretch the truth for *fun* like Dad. I did it because I had no choice. The other third graders had cool stories to tell for real. But when you're nobody special, the truth needs a little help.

It was different last year. Second grade was like a great big happy party, and we were all invited. A baboon could feel special in Grade Two.

But third grade was all times-tables and computers and books with hardly any pictures. It was hard. And I stunk at most of it. If I didn't make stuff up, I'd be the world champion loser for sure.

I asked one last time, "So am I in trouble, or what?"

"Not if you think carefully about what

I said," replied Dr. Bradley. "And don't forget my note. Now hurry back to class. Mrs. Moore is showing a science film on eagles."

What?!

I couldn't believe my bad luck. Videos are the best thing about Mrs. Moore's class. As soon as she turns out the lights, we pretend we're in a real movie theater. Sometimes we even get popcorn to eat during the show.

Maybe the film wasn't over yet. Maybe there was still some popcorn left!

I practically launched myself out of the office. I was running down the hall so fast that I shot right past Brittany outside our classroom.

"It's too late," she called to me. "You missed the video."

I stopped in my tracks. I tried to tell myself that the film wasn't any good.

Eagles. Who cared about a bunch of dumb old eagles?

"Lousy video, huh?" I said hopefully. "I mean, science, how boring can you get?"

"Are you kidding?" she cried. "It was the best film all year! We got to see how eagles make their nests, and have babies, and everything. And the popcorn was caramel flavored."

My favorite. "No fair —" I began.

Then I noticed Brittany was wearing her gym shorts. She carried her skirt draped over her arm.

"Hey," I asked. "How come you changed clothes?"

"We're all going to draw pictures of an eagle's nest," she explained. "I can't risk getting crayon on my new skirt."

I frowned. "Why not?"

She looked at me like I was from Mars. "This isn't just any old skirt!" she exclaimed. "It's a *designer* skirt. A Sergio Labanza original, imported all the way from Italy. It's made of Ultra-Soft Anti-Static Never-Wrinkle cotton!"

She held it up right in my face. It looked like a regular plain old skirt to me.

All I could think of was, "Oh."

Brittany pointed to the envelope in my hand. "Is that a note from the principal?"

I was *dying* to say no. But lying had just landed me in Dr. Bradley's office. Thanks to my big mouth, I had just missed the greatest video in the history of school.

"Yeah," I admitted.

"Ha, ha, ha!" she guffawed at me. "You're in big trouble now —"

"I am not!" I interrupted.

Lying had landed me in the soup, but telling the truth was even worse. How could I confess my problems to Brittany, the prettiest and most popular girl in school?

Why, her *clothes* sounded cooler than my entire life! If she blabbed about my note to the class, I'd never hear the end of it.

"Check it out," I began. "Sure, this is a note from Dr. Bradley — a *thank-you* note. When he found out my family has a nuclear toilet, he wanted to know where he could buy one for his house. *That's* why I got called to the office."

"No way," said Brittany.

"Yes, way!"

"Prove it," Brittany challenged.

She grabbed the envelope and tried to pull it out of my hands. I hung on.

"Let me see the note!" she grunted.

"Lay off!" I shot back.

It was like a tug-of-war, only with a letter instead of a rope. Then, all at once, Brittany let go.

I went flying — straight through the open doorway of our class!

chapter three

A Real Eagle's Nest

I stumbled backward into the room. Right in front of everybody, I tripped over my own feet. With a crash, I landed in a heap on the floor. Dr. Bradley's note was still clutched in my hands.

The class laughed at me. Some of them still had caramel popcorn crumbs around their mouths.

The teacher switched off the VCR. She looked at me. "Zoe, what on *earth* are you doing?"

Brittany stepped into the doorway. "Mrs. Moore, Zoe is lying again. She's lying about getting in trouble for lying."

"I am not!" I defended myself. "*You're* lying about me lying about lying!"

Even I didn't understand *that.* And I was the one who said it.

"Take your seats, both of you," ordered Mrs. Moore.

I sat down next to Michael Rothman. Michael was the quietest kid in our class. He had these really big eyes, like car headlights.

Now the headlights were on me.

"I'm not lying!" I snapped at him.

"I never said you were," he replied softly.

"Now, Zoe," said Mrs. Moore, "we're all drawing pictures of an eagle's nest. Since you missed the film, you may draw whatever you like."

I pulled a sheet of art paper out of my

desk. "I can draw just as good an eagle's nest as anybody here," I said angrily.

"No way!"

Guess who? Jerry Paradise.

"You can*not!*" Jerry challenged me. "You don't even know what an eagle's nest looks like."

"I do so," I shot back.

"Do not! Do not!" He sounded like a parrot. Except parrots are a lot smarter than Jerry.

"You missed the film," added Brittany. "You've never seen an eagle's nest."

"I've seen an eagle's nest millions of times," I blurted out.

"Yeah? Where?" asked Jerry.

This was another one of those moments when the truth needed a little help.

A *lot* of help.

"Check it out," I began. "There's a real

eagle's nest right in my backyard. I can look at it anytime I want."

"Ha! I got you!" cried Jerry. He waved his hand wildly at the teacher. "Mrs. Moore? The video said that eagles only make their nests in *high* places. Right? Right, Mrs. Moore?"

"That's correct, Jerry," Mrs. Moore approved.

The teacher turned to me. She definitely didn't look happy. "Zoe, are you *sure* about this? Eagles' nests are very rare. Especially where there are houses and people."

"It's in my backyard, *way* up in the tallest tree," I insisted. "Here. I'll draw it for you."

Michael was looking at me with those big eyes again. He said, "It wasn't that good."

"What wasn't?" I asked.

"The video. You didn't miss much."

He held out his drawing to me. "Do you want to see what the nest looks like?"

"I *know* what the nest looks like, doofus," I replied. "I see one every day, remember?"

He said nothing. But he pushed his paper over to the side of his desk, where I could see it.

Michael was the best artist in our class. It wasn't easy to copy his drawing. My picture looked more like a bowl of soup than a nest. Then I drew an eagle that kind of resembled Barney the dinosaur, only uglier.

I stink at art. I once did a portrait of my dad, and everybody thought it was a tulip with a mustache.

At the end of the day, I handed in my drawing.

"See?" I announced to Mrs. Moore. "I told you there's a nest in my backyard."

She just sighed. It was pretty obvious she didn't believe me.

Nobody else did either. In the school yard, the other third graders formed a circle around me. They flapped their arms and made eagle noises and laughed at me.

This never would have happened in second grade.

Jerry ripped Dr. Bradley's note out of my pocket. "Now we'll see who's in trouble!" he cheered.

"Give that back!" I shouted.

I reached for the envelope, but Jerry held it high up above my grasp.

Suddenly, a hand reached out behind Jerry. It snatched away the note and tossed it into my arms.

"Who did that?" cried Jerry.

We all stared. It was Michael.

What was he doing? He was getting everyone mad at him for no reason.

Just my luck. Not only did my whole class hate me, but I had the desk right next to a weirdo.

While Jerry was yelling at Michael, I tried to sneak away from the group.

"Hey!" exclaimed Kevin. "She's getting away!"

I broke into a run. Kevin, Jerry, Brittany, and Gary Galonsky chased after me.

It was no use. Kevin was the fastest kid in the third grade. He'd catch me, and then Gary would beat me up if I didn't give them the note. Everybody was afraid of Gary, even Kevin. Maybe even the fifth graders.

I looked over my shoulder. They were gaining on me! My breath was coming out in gasps.

Then I remembered — *the shortcut!*

Desperately, I ducked into the Abernathy's yard. I hid behind the shed and peeked out. Kevin, Jerry, Brittany, and Gary ran right past the house. I'd lost them.

I climbed over the fence, and dropped to the ground in my own backyard.

Safe!

I took Dr. Bradley's note out of my pocket. I sure wasn't going to give it to Dad. Then I'd be in even more trouble. But it wasn't safe to take it back to school again. Not anymore. And I couldn't just throw it out. Mom might notice it in the garbage. I needed to get rid of this letter for good. But how?

Then it hit me.

What made our house different from every other house in the whole world?

chapter four

There's No Trust in Third Grade

SPLOOOOOOOOSH!!

No, it wasn't a tidal wave.

It was the sound of the nuclear toilet flushing down the principal's note. If you wanted something to disappear, the nuclear toilet was better than a real magician. Deep-sea divers armed with Roto-Rooters couldn't find that letter now.

"Zo? What are you doing?"

Oh, no. It was Joey.

"It's a bathroom," I answered. "What do you think I'm doing?"

He laughed like I had just told the funniest joke in history.

"Yeah, sure — with the door open!" he said at last. "You flushed something. It looked like an envelope."

I put an arm around Joey's shoulders. "Check it out," I began. "I had to get rid of that envelope. It had the code names of all the enemy secret agents."

It was fun to watch his eyes become as wide as saucers. "Wow! Cool!"

The best thing about having a little brother was that he believed everything that came out of my mouth. He looked up to me. Even though I was the class joke, I always felt important when Joey was around.

I nodded seriously. "The enemy agents would kill me if they knew I had the list. And then they'd have to kill you, too, because you know too much. And probably Mom and Dad."

Joey was really terrified. "But what were you doing with secret code names?"

I thought fast. "I'm doing a project on secret agents for school."

"Whoa!" Joey was as pale as a ghost. "Maybe you better flush it again, just to make sure it's all the way gone!"

"Don't worry," I said. "When the nuclear toilet flushes something, it stays flushed."

Joey looked nervous. "I don't think I'm going to like third grade. It sounds kind of scary."

I gave him my most mature look. "It's rough," I agreed. "There's no trust in third grade. Like, if I told you we had an eagle's nest in the backyard, you'd take my word for it, right?"

He brightened. "We have an eagle's nest in the backyard?"

See? The kid would believe me if I told him the world was made of coleslaw.

Have you got the List?
Yeah. Right here. In my briefcase...

"Of course not," I said. "Jeez, Joey. Get a grip."

He was really confused. "So why did you say we did?"

"The point is," I told him, "*you* listen to me. At school, those jerks just laughed when I said there was an eagle's nest in our backyard."

Joey thought hard. "Well, maybe if you took a *picture* of the nest —"

Then he remembered. "Oh, yeah. There *is* no nest. Sorry, Zo."

"No, wait," I said.

After all, this was the kid who had pulled straight A's since nursery school. This was the next Albert What's-his-face. Grandpa was right. He *was* a genius!

"That's a great idea!" I cried. "A real picture would *prove* that we have a nest."

"But we don't," Joey said.

"But we *will*."

chapter five

Eagles Don't Like Peanut Butter

Mom's electric wok was exactly nest-shaped. And just the right size.

"That's for cooking," Joey protested.

I took it out of the cupboard. It was perfect.

"Mom will never let you use it," said Joey. "She's going to say no."

"Bet a week's TV picks?" I challenged.

This was a hefty bet. The winner would be in charge of

the remote control when Mom and Dad weren't around.

"Done."

We sealed the deal with our official handshake. We bonked fists up and down, side and side.

"I'm going to win!" crowed Joey.

"You're going to *lose,*" I told him. "Mom can't say no if I don't ask her. And I'm not planning to."

Joey looked miserable. I had bamboozled him again.

"Hey, cheer up," I said. "If you come and help me collect leaves, I promise we'll watch a couple of your shows."

We went out to the backyard.

Joey wanted to yank all the leaves off the first tree we saw.

"Think, Joe," I told him. "Mom and Dad

will kill us if they come home and find a totally naked tree."

We took a few leaves from each tree until our shopping bag was half full. I tossed in sticks and twigs, and soon it was loaded to the top. Then came the hard part—attaching all that junk to Mom's wok. I used up a lot of Elmer's glue. I had to do most of the work myself, since Joey wasn't allowed to touch the glue anymore.

Last year I told Joey it was shampoo, and he tried to wash his hair with it. It made a pretty amazing mess, and then it hardened. He had to have his head shaved to get rid of it.

But I made him feel better. I told him the bald look was cool. Naturally, he believed me.

Mom and Dad were harder to convince. By the time they got through with me, I would have been happy to trade places with my brother the chrome-dome.

So I was in charge of gluing on the leaves. It was the most important job. After all, I couldn't show Mrs. Moore and Jerry and Brittany and Michael and everybody a picture of an eagle's nest with *E-Z Wok* printed on the side.

So I pasted a giant maple leaf over the label. A pinecone covered the temperature knob. A thick twig covered the on-off switch.

I ran out of glue so I switched to Scotch tape. Then I ran out of tape.

"Here," said Joey. "Use this." He held up a jar of peanut butter.

"Are you out of your mind?" I cried. "What kind of an eagle builds its nest out of peanut butter?"

He looked hurt. His lower lip quivered. He said, "I love peanut butter."

ON
OFF
PEANUT

"Yeah, but eagles probably don't," I reminded him.

"How do you know?" he asked.

"Oh, all right." After all, this was *his* idea.

It was definitely sticky enough. Maybe the kid was onto something.

The last few leaves went on with Jif Extra Crunchy.

chapter six

Go Climb a Tree

"How come the nest has to go way up in a tree?" asked Joey.

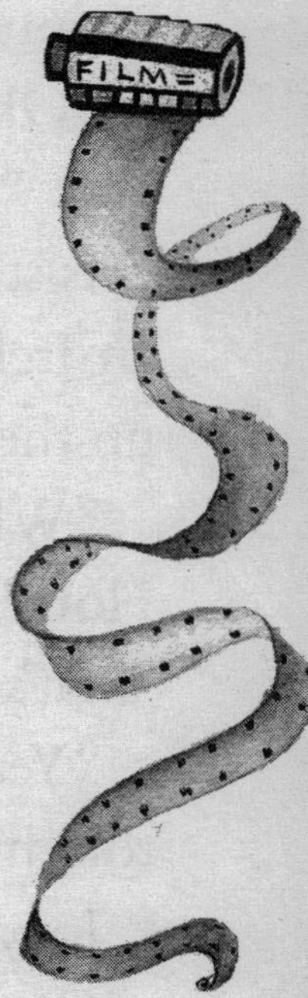

"It's for an eagle, not an earthworm," I told him. "It has to be *high*."

I looked around the backyard. Our trees were kind of puny for an eagle's nest — even a fake one made out of an electric wok.

The weeping willow was the best. It wasn't the tallest. But it had big sturdy limbs.

I huddled with Joey.

"Okay," I said, "when you're climbing, remember to keep one hand on the tree and one hand on the wok. I mean, the nest."

"*Me?*" he cried. "Why me?"

"Check it out," I began. "I'd love to be the climber, but I'm allergic to gravity."

"Really?" He looked scared. "Is it serious?"

"Oh, here on the ground I'm fine," I said. "But when I go up high, the gravity gets stronger. I get hives, and I break out in an itchy rash. If my throat closes halfway up the tree, I could die."

"What about the time we went to Florida?" Joey asked. "We were in a *plane*. That's way higher than a tree."

"Yeah, but I had to get allergy shots," I told him. "Really long needles."

Joey started up the trunk like a monkey.

On tiptoe, I handed him the nest. He took it and crawled out on a branch.

"Make sure the cord doesn't show," I coached him. "Who ever heard of an electric eagle's nest?"

He saluted and almost dropped the nest.

"Careful," I called. "If you fall, you'll break the wok, and Mom will kill us."

He teetered on the branch. "If I fall," he said nervously, "I'll already be dead."

"Careful!"

I stepped forward to catch the wok. But that wasn't what I caught. Instead, *Joey* tumbled from the branch into my arms.

His weight knocked me over. The two of us ended up flat on our backs in the grass.

"Where's the wok? Where's the nest?" I cried.

We both looked up. We saw it at the same time.

The wok was still in the tree. It was

perfectly balanced. It looked like it *belonged* there.

"It's awesome!" crowed Joey. "It's just like a real eagle's nest."

"You've never seen an eagle's nest," I reminded him.

"Oh, right," he said. "Have you?"

I nodded. "In class we saw a whole film about them."

I didn't tell him that I was sharpening pencils while everyone else was munching on caramel popcorn.

Besides, I knew in my heart what an eagle's nest looked like. It looked exactly like Mom's wok, covered with leaves, in our weeping willow tree.

I ran like crazy and got my dad's camera. I was already shooting pictures when I burst back out the door.

This was it! My eagle's nest! When Mrs.

Moore and the others saw these pictures, everything would be different.

Brittany would forget about my note from the principal. Jerry would stop tattling on me. Nobody would laugh, or flap their arms, or chase me home from school.

Click! Click! Click! Click!

I must have hit the button a hundred times.

"Hey, Zo," said Joey. "Didn't Dad use up all the film during Grandpa's last visit?"

"What? Oh, no!" I checked the camera.

Out of film.

chapter seven

Raw Fish

The next morning, right after breakfast, my father took me aside. He laid a soggy paper on the table in front of me.

I stared at the wet page. The writing had faded into blotches of blue ink. It was impossible to read a single word.

"What is it?" I asked.

"I lost a cuff link down the nuclear toilet," Dad told me. "This came up while I was plunging."

Dr. Bradley's note.

I remembered all of the things that had been flushed away forever — earrings, toothbrushes, pencils, money, an alarm clock, soap, and even one of Joey's shoes when he was a baby. A flimsy little letter should have been halfway to China by now!

But maybe the nuclear toilet wasn't as nuclear as I thought.

Dad pointed to the paper. *Elmwood School* was smeared across the top. "What do you know about this, Zoe?"

"Check it out," I said. "I just got voted student of the month. Dr. Bradley probably wanted to congratulate you and Mom on what a great job you did raising me."

Dad didn't look too impressed. "And how did the note get into the toilet?"

I thought fast. "Ants," I said quickly. "An army of ants must have carried it down the table leg, through the kitchen, and into the bathroom."

He laughed out loud. "Ha! That's a good one. I never would have thought of ants."

I love cracking up my father. He has one of those deep belly laughs that fills up a room.

Then he turned serious again. He put an arm around my shoulders. "Dr. Bradley never sends a note home for something *good*. I should know. He used to be my teacher."

"He said some terrible things about you, Dad," I told him. "He said you used to lie all the time."

"It's true," Dad admitted.

"Really?" I was shocked. "You said Grandma was a parachute jumper, and Grandpa was an ambassador?"

Dad nodded. "He left out the time I told him Uncle Jeff was Nodrog Namrok, Master Trainer of the Ninjas."

I couldn't believe my ears. "Well, even if

it's all true, couldn't we still, like, sue him for saying such mean things?"

He looked straight into my eyes. "Zoe, I know it's fun to make up stories. But you can't just lie whenever you want to impress somebody. Remember, it's what you've got *inside* that makes people like you."

"But what if what's inside *me* isn't any good?" I asked.

Dad smiled. "It is. Trust me. Cut you open and you'll find lots and lots of terrific and wonderful. And not a single speck of lousy."

That gave me an idea.

"Since I've got so much good stuff," I said, "how about buying me a new roll of film for the camera?"

Dad raised one of his eyebrows. "Does this have anything to do with the letter you *didn't* flush down the nuclear toilet?"

"We're doing a unit on leaves in school,"

I told him. "I want to bring in pictures of the different kinds of trees in our backyard."

"I thought your class was studying eagles," he reminded me.

"Right." My mind raced. "But when eagles land in trees, where are they? In the middle of a bunch of leaves."

He looked suspicious. I got this weird feeling in the pit of my stomach. Here was Dad, trying to be nice.

And I lied to him.

But he was wrong about one thing. Lying was no fun at all. In fact, it was getting to be hard work.

I had to lie just to keep all my other lies from blowing up in my face.

Every Wednesday at school, our class had "Sharing."

Jerry Paradise always went first. Not

because it was a rule, but because he had a mouth bigger than the Grand Canyon.

"My dad called from Japan last night," he blabbed. "Of course, it wasn't night *there*. It was breakfast time. He says it's the coolest place in the whole world. They have trains that go as fast as airplanes. And nobody shakes hands — they *bow*. And they eat everything with chopsticks — even spaghetti! Yesterday my dad had sushi for dinner. Guess what that is — raw fish!"

"Yeccch!" chorused half the class.

I raised my hand. "Mrs. Moore, this isn't fair. How come I get in trouble for lying, but it's okay for Jerry? I mean, raw fish! Give me a break."

"Sushi is considered a delicacy in Japan," Mrs. Moore told me. "And many people enjoy it in our country as well."

"Yeah, right," I snorted with a laugh. "Like who?"

The teacher fixed me with a hard stare. "Like me."

Jerry smiled his nasty *I-told-you-so* smile. "See? Look who's making fun of me. The biggest liar in the universe!"

I'll bet my face was bright red. "I am not, and I can prove it. My dad is going to buy film, so I'll have a picture of my eagle's nest really, really soon."

I thought the class would be impressed. Instead, they started flapping their arms at me again.

"Liar, liar, pants on fire!" shouted Jerry.

I felt sick. How come I could never seem to do or say the right thing?

I was so upset, I couldn't even fight back.

"Mrs. Moore, make them stop," I pleaded. My voice was barely as loud as a whisper.

"Quiet, everybody!" the teacher ordered. To me she said softly, "I'm so sorry, Zoe.

LIAR!
HA!
HA!
LIAR!
HA!
LIAR!
HA!
HA!
LIAR!
HA!
LIAR!
HA!
Sorry ZOE.

But this is what happens when you don't tell the truth."

But I knew that Mrs. Moore couldn't be more wrong.

If my classmates were this rotten to me *now,* telling the truth would only make it worse. Because then everybody would know what a zero I was.

Zoe Bent, nobody special in a world of somebodies.

chapter eight

Safe or Out?

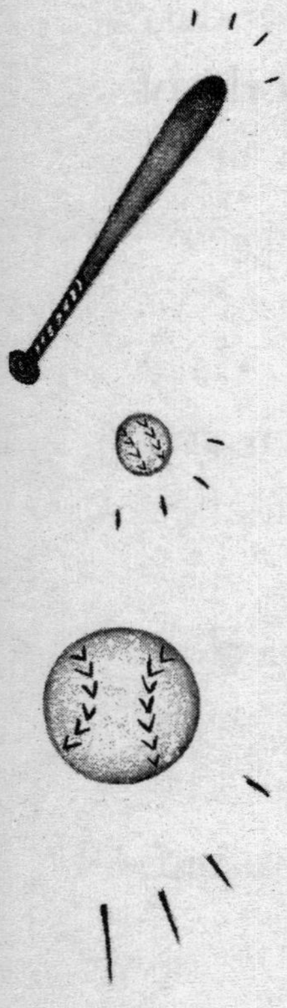

Just when I thought things couldn't get worse, we played softball in gym. I stink at softball even worse than I stink at art — which is a whole lot. Most miserable of all, I got stuck playing catcher.

I hate being the catcher. Last time, I went into my crouch and my shorts split right up the back. I spent the rest of P.E. holding my glove behind me so the whole class wouldn't see my underwear.

Today the score was tied 3–3. Brittany got a hit. Gary Galonsky came charging in from third base. If he touched home plate, the game would be over. We would lose 4–3.

Kevin dove for the ball. He picked it up and threw it to me. Big Gary was coming at me like a freight train. The whole class was yelling and screaming. I could feel my heart pounding in my throat. If I messed up, they'd all have one more reason to hate me.

The ball thumped into my glove. Gary was starting to slide. I reached down and tagged him out *just* before he touched home!

He jumped to his feet. "Safe!" he cried.

"Safe?!" I repeated. "You're out! I *tagged* you!"

"*After* I slid into home plate," he insisted.

"No!"

Mrs. Moore came up. "What's the problem here?"

"I was safe," Gary told her.

"You were *out,*" I corrected.

She looked at us. She was deciding who to believe. She was thinking about all the stories I had made up. All the times I'd stretched the truth.

Okay, I admit it. All the lies.

"Gary is safe," she announced.

"What?" I cried. "No fair! I tagged him!"

"We won!" cheered Brittany.

The other team picked up Gary and carried him around on their shoulders. He waved his arms like a champion.

My teammates wouldn't even look at me.

"Way to go, Zoe," mumbled Kevin.

"But I got him," I said. "He was out."

"Sure he was," sneered Jerry. "And I'm the president of the United States."

ZOE'S BIG MOUTH

We started back for the school. I had one last hope.

"What a rip-off," I told Michael Rothman. "Gary was out."

He said, "It looked pretty close, Zoe."

"Aw, come on!" I pleaded. "You've got the biggest eyes in the world. What good are they if you can't even see a tag in softball?"

Michael shrugged and kept on walking.

I wanted to shriek the whole school down: *But it's true! It's not like all those other times when I was making it up. I tagged him. Honest!*

Of course, then I'd have to confess to a thousand lies from before.

I was trapped by my own big mouth.

chapter nine

An Unexpected Visitor

As soon as I got home, I ran straight upstairs to my room. What a day. I was almost as exhausted as I was miserable.

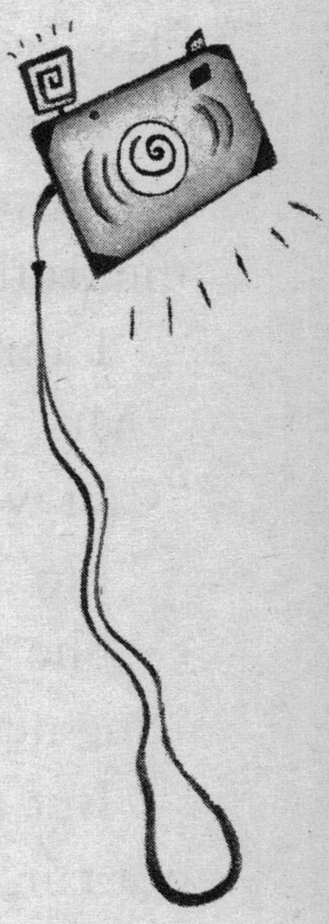

I climbed into bed and pulled the covers right up to my nostrils. Soon I dozed off. I dreamed that I was back in school. Even asleep, I couldn't escape my third-grade class.

In the dream, Mrs. Moore was calling the roll. But when I said, "Here," Jerry Paradise screamed out, "Liar, liar, pants on fire!"

I couldn't believe my ears. "What?"

The teacher frowned at me. "You're not Zoe Bent."

"Of course I am," I said in surprise. "You know me."

"That's not Zoe," Brittany told Mrs. Moore. "That's some other girl."

"She's not even supposed to be in this class," added Kevin.

"But it's *me!*" I pleaded.

"How can we be sure you're telling us the truth?" asked Michael.

"I am! I *swear.*"

Mrs. Moore looked around the room. "Can we trust her?"

"No!" shouted at least ten people.

"She lies all the time," piped up Jerry. "She never tells the truth."

"But that's not right," I babbled. "That's not fair."

"Well, let's see," the teacher began. "You

said you met a movie star on the way to school. Was that true?"

"Well — no," I admitted.

"And you said you have an eagle's nest in your backyard," she went on. "Do you?"

"No," I murmured.

"You lie to your little brother all the time. You even lied to your father. Right?"

"Yes." I was so ashamed, I couldn't even look at anyone.

"So why should we believe you now?" chorused everybody.

The words rang in my ears, crashing and clattering like —

"Zoe!" called my mom. From the kitchen came the rattle of pots and pans. "Have you seen the electric wok?"

Uh-oh.

Her wok wasn't a wok anymore. It was an eagle's nest in a willow tree. And it was covered with leaves and glue and sticks and tape and peanut butter.

This time the truth needed more than a little help. It needed a miracle.

"Check it out," I yelled to her. "I — uh — I — I'm going outside!"

I crept downstairs on tiptoe. I snuck past the kitchen and ran out the back door.

I gazed up at my beautiful eagle's nest.

"Nobody is ever going to see you," I said to it, "because Mom wants to use you to stir-fry a bunch of gross vegetables."

My eyes filled with tears. It was stupid, I knew. It wasn't even a real eagle's nest. But in a way, it was more important than the best and biggest real nest of all time. It was my chance to be somebody special.

Now that would be gone. And nobody would believe me, or like me ever again.

Suddenly, a dark shape appeared in the sky. It grew larger and larger. It was a bird.

A *giant* bird.

I stared. Each wing was as big as I was. It circled over the willow tree. Then it landed on the branch right next to Mom's wok. I gasped.

It was an eagle. A real eagle!

It looked nothing like Barney the dinosaur. It looked just like the picture on Express Mail, only fifty times more wonderful! Its crown was as white as cotton balls. It reached its head into the wok. When it came out, its beak was smeared with brown.

The eagle was eating the peanut butter!

I heard a car door slam. My dad. The film! I sprinted around to the front of the house.

"Hi, Zoe —" Dad greeted.

I snatched the film out of his hand without a word. I darted inside and loaded the camera.

YUM! PEANUT BUTTER!

“Zoe —” my mother called.

I ignored her, too. I had no time to spare. I rocketed out back.

The eagle was still there, snacking on peanut butter out of Mom’s wok. I aimed the camera. I shot all twenty-four pictures of the eagle in our willow tree.

When I ran out of film, I cheered, “Oh, thank you, thank you, thank you!”

Who needed lies when you had a real honest-to-goodness eagle right in your own backyard? When my class saw these pictures, all my troubles would be over. I would be the hero of the third grade!

The eagle finished its dinner. As it spread its wings to fly away, it knocked the wok off the branch.

“Oh, no!” I cried.

I dove forward to catch it, but I slipped. I landed flat on my face by the base of the tree. The wok bounced off my behind. It came to rest in the grass beside me. By now, my eagle friend was just a tiny dot in the sky.

Joey came running out to me. His face was white.

"Mom's looking for the wok, Zoe!" he whined. "She's searching the whole house!"

"Don't panic. Remember — we're in this together."

"In your dreams!" he said, and ran back inside.

So much for brotherly love.

I turned to my eagle's nest. I ripped away all the leaves and sticks and tape.

I stared in horror. There were still gobs of glue everywhere, with bits of stem and twig stuck here and there. I scratched at the glue. It was as solid as a jawbreaker.

There was only one force in nature powerful enough to clean the wok.

The nuclear toilet.

I snuck in the back door on tiptoe. I held the wok straight out in front of me. I couldn't risk banging it against a wall or a chair. Mom would hear the noise.

I could see the downstairs bathroom ahead of me. Just three more steps! I reached for the door.

An unfriendly hand clamped on my shoulder.

"Zoe Michelle Bent," came my mother's voice.

Caught!

chapter ten

Major, Major Trouble

To say I got in trouble would be like saying the Pacific Ocean was a little wet.

I got in major, major trouble. Mom chewed me out and sent me to my room. Then she came up there, banned me from the TV, chewed me out some more, and grounded me. She also took away my allowance until I am thirty.

I don't think seventy-five cents a week will buy much in the year 2018.

Early the next morning, there was a knock at my door. Maybe Mom needed to get in a few last licks.

"I'm sick," I moaned. "I have hoof-and-mouth disease. And it's highly contagious."

My dad came in. He wore a sympathetic smile. He sat down beside me on the bed.

"Only cows get hoof-and-mouth disease," he told me.

"I think a sick cow coughed in my face," I said.

He put an arm around my shoulders. "Rough night, huh?"

I shuddered. "A rough night is when there's boring stuff on Nickelodeon."

He laughed. "I called Dr. Bradley yesterday."

Oh, no. Just when I thought things couldn't get any worse. I barely had the guts to ask the question. "What did he say?"

"He thinks you're a great kid," Dad said seriously.

"No way," I blurted out. "I mean — uh — that's it? Nothing else?" Nothing about how I was a terrible liar and all my classmates hated me?

"We only talked for a few minutes," Dad admitted. "Remember, Zoe, it's what's *inside* that makes people like you. Dr. Bradley sees all that good stuff you've got deep down."

He smiled. "I took your film over to Fotomat last night. I figured we could pick up the pictures on the way to school today." He paused. "But if you're not feeling well —"

He couldn't finish because I was hugging him too hard.

The school bell rang.

It was faint, but I knew what it was. I

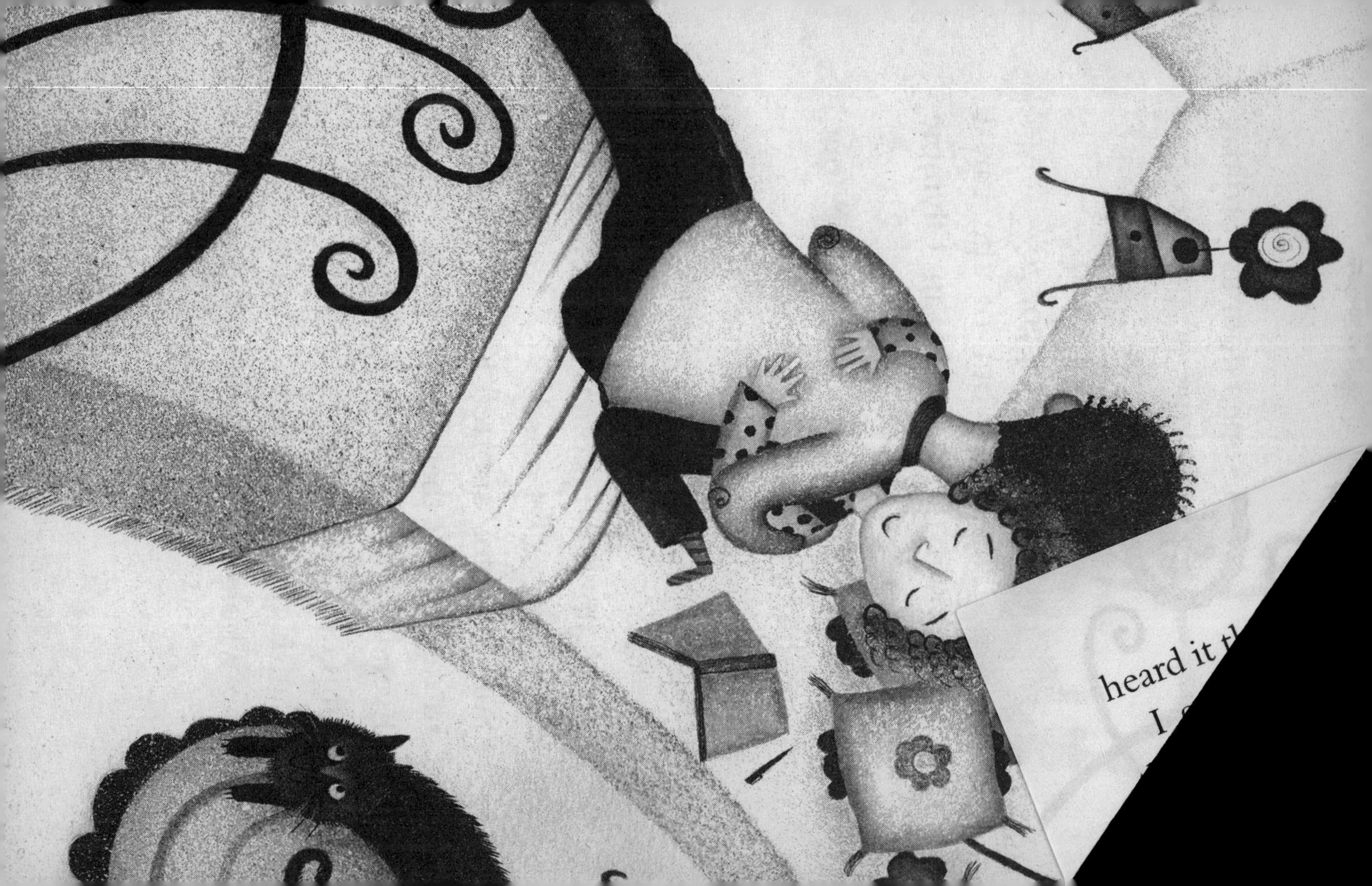

heard it t
I

hrough the open door at Fotomat. grabbed my envelope of pictures and threw myself into Dad's car.

"How do they look?" he asked.

"No time!" I cried. "Go, go, go!"

At school, I leaped out of the car. I sprinted down the hall like an Olympic champion.

I got to class in time to gasp out, ". . . with liberty and justice for all."

Mrs. Moore frowned at me. "I suppose you have another wild story to explain why you're late."

I held up the Fotomat envelope. "I've got the pictures!" I cried.

"Sure you do," snorted Kevin. "Pictures of an eagle's nest that doesn't exist."

"Even better than that," I raved. "I've got pictures of a real eagle!"

"Liar, liar, pants on fire!" shouted Jerry.

The whole class gathered around. Even

Mrs. Moore. I was the center of attention.

My hands were trembling with excitement. I pulled out the pictures.

Kevin pointed to the top photo. "Hey, what's that?"

All you could see was a big pink blur.

"Oh," I laughed. "I guess I got my thumb in front of the camera for that one."

I moved on to the second picture. My thumb again. And the third. And the fourth.

I was starting to panic. I sorted through the rest of the envelope. Twenty-four pictures of my thumb.

"Oh, *no!*" I cried. "No! No! *No!* You can't see the eagle!"

A roar of laughter went up in the classroom. Giggles. Chuckles. Snickers. Guffaws.

"There never was any eagle," sneered Jerry. "Just like there never was any nest."

"Yes, there was," I babbled. "Right there behind my thumb. Honest."

Mrs. Moore shook her head at me. "Sit down, Zoe."

I would not sit down. "But it's true. One hundred percent, absolutely, good-as-gold, totally true."

The class started flapping at me worse than ever. It was a flap-a-thon.

Michael was the only non-flapper. I looked into those big eyes. "You believe me, right?"

He rolled them at me. "Oh, grow up."

Nobody believed me — *and I wasn't even lying.*

I was worse than nobody special. I was nobody, *period.*

chapter eleven

Somebody Special

It was the worst time of my whole life.

It was the sludge from the darkest corner of the slime pit of misery. I wasn't even happy that it was the weekend. Home was no better than school.

Mom hadn't forgiven me for killing the wok. I was fighting with Joey for letting me take the blame alone. Dad was upset because I wasted a whole roll of film.

If we had a dog, I bet it would

hate me, too. Same with a hamster, or even a goldfish. If we had a totally disgusting vampire bat, it would probably love me.

I spent Saturday moping around my room. I looked out the window at our willow tree. I could even see the branch where Mom's wok had once sat.

And then something moved.

I stared. Somebody was in our backyard.

I opened the window and called, "Hey, you!"

He turned around. Huge eyes gazed up at me. It was Michael.

My heart leaped. Was he coming to see me?

Then I remembered. Michael was crazy. He might do almost anything. Even visit a loser like me.

I ran downstairs and out the back door.

"What are you doing here?" I asked him.

"I was wrong not to believe you yesterday," he told me. "Maybe you really do have an eagle's nest."

Sure, he was crazy. But I wanted him to like me. I wanted *anybody* to like me. "Yeah?" I said.

"So could I see it?" he asked.

But there was no more nest to show.

"Check it out," I began. "The eagle found a better tree. It's taller, with a great view, and there are lots more mice to hunt in that neighborhood. So he moved his nest over there."

Michael's face fell. He didn't look very crazy to me. He looked like he knew I was lying, and he was hurt.

I thought back to all the times that Michael had stuck up for me. Talked to me when nobody else would. Why, he risked getting the whole class mad at him just to help me. And I hadn't even noticed.

Now he was here to give me one last chance.

It hit me like a runaway train. *Michael wasn't crazy at all. He was trying to be my friend.*

I felt my heart twist. Of all the kids in school, Michael was the only one who could see the good stuff I had inside. And I let him down.

"I lied," I admitted. "There never was any nest. It was just my mom's wok with a few leaves on it."

He nodded. "So there wasn't any eagle?"

"That part's true," I said quickly. "I stuck the leaves on the wok with peanut butter. That's why the eagle came. To eat the peanut butter."

His eyes cut through me like lasers. He might as well have been Jerry Paradise. I could almost hear it: *Liar, liar, pants on fire!*

I felt terrible and confused. Lying was

wrong. But the truth wasn't working either.

Suddenly, Michael reached down to the grass and picked something up. At first I thought it was a leaf. But it was dark gray.

He cupped it in both hands. It was a long feather.

An eagle feather!

He stared in amazement. His mouth formed an O. "Is this —?"

"Yeah!" I cried.

Please believe me.

But I could see it in his eyes. He wasn't sure.

Michael handed me the feather. "Well, I should get home. Could I please use your bathroom before I go?"

"Yeah, okay," I mumbled. "Straight down the hall. Turn right."

I ushered him in through the screen door. He disappeared around the corner.

I ran my fingers up and down the feather. I felt like crying.

Michael and I could have been great friends. But he didn't want to hang out with a liar. And who could blame him?

I almost screamed, *You're right! The feather was fake! There was no eagle!* But that would have been lying, too.

I made a decision. No more stretching the truth. No more wild stories. One friend was one too many to lose over *nothing*.

I heard a familiar roar.

Suddenly, Michael came running down the hall. His mouth hung open in shock. His eyes were even wider than usual.

I stuffed the feather in my pocket.

"Michael, what's wrong?"

He was pointing toward the downstairs bathroom.

"You — you —" he stammered, "— you really *do* have a nuclear toilet!"

"Nuclear as an atomic bomb," I nodded.

You could see it in his eyes: If the nuclear toilet was true, then maybe, just maybe . . .

He looked at me. "You saw a real eagle?"

I nodded. "I know it sounds crazy. But it happened."

"Wow," he said. "Eagles like peanut butter."

"I wonder if it sticks to the roof of their beaks," I joked.

We both laughed.

"Maybe if you didn't make up so much crazy stuff," Michael said, "people would believe you when you really *are* telling the truth."

"But if I didn't make up stuff," I complained, "I'd never have anything to say."

He frowned. "What are you talking about?"

"You're great at art," I told him. "Brittany wears all the cool clothes. Kevin's good at sports. Jerry's family travels all over the world. Gary is really strong. My brother is a genius." I studied my sneakers. "I stink at everything."

"But, Zoe!" he cried. "Don't you get it? You've got a talent that *none* of us can match."

I folded my arms in front of me. "What?"

"You have the greatest imagination in the history of third grade!" Michael exclaimed.

As soon as he said it, I knew it was right. It just seemed to fit me, like one of Brittany's designer skirts. Nobody could invent things like I could. I just had to stop myself from telling people they were true.

Amazing! *I* was somebody special.

I had a superstar imagination — just like Dad!

"You're right!" I crowed. "Michael, you're awesome!"

I was *twice* as special because I had a friend like Michael. Someone who supported me and stuck by me in good times and bad.

We had a lot of bad these last few days. But I could see a giant humongous load of good starting right now.

And when I told Michael what great friends we were going to be, his big eyes sparkled. Because he totally believed me.

When you're somebody special, the truth doesn't need any help at all.

About the Author

Gordon Korman has always been a good inventor of excuses, so creating Zoe and all her zany lies came naturally to him. But the nuclear toilet in Zoe's house is one hundred percent true. Gordon actually saw one during a school visit in California. When he isn't traveling, Gordon makes up all kinds of stories for middle-grade and young-adult readers. He and his wife live in New York City and Toronto, Canada. Honest.

About the Illustrator

JoAnn Adinolfi always told the truth when she was growing up, but she got into trouble anyway. She has illustrated five picture books, most recently one called *Tina's Diner*. She and her husband live in a big penthouse apartment in Manhattan with eleven dogs, a rooftop garden, and a giant studio overlooking the Hudson River. Is that a lie? "Just a fantasy," she promises.

Join

The Friendship Ring

Rachel Vail

a new series for girls

Meet Zoe, CJ, Morgan, and Olivia

Books the same size as CD's!

If You Only Knew

Please, Please, Please

Not That I Care

What Are Friends For?
Coming in February 1999

SCHOLASTIC

FRI6

Plunging into adventure again!

CAPTAIN UNDERPANTS

and the Attack of the Talking Toilets

by Dav Pilkey

Watch out world—because big briefs are back!

Coming to bookstores in January!